Healthy Me

Mental Well-being and Mindfulness

Ryan Wheatcroft   Katie Woolley

WAYLAND

Published in paperback in Great Britain in 2019 by Wayland

Copyright © Hodder and Stoughton, 2018

Editor: Victoria Brooker
Designer: Anthony Hannant, Little Red Ant

ISBN: 978 1 5263 0564 0

10 9 8 7 6 5 4

Wayland, an imprint of
Hachette Children's Group
Part of Hodder and Stoughton
Carmelite House
50 Victoria Embankment
London EC4Y 0DZ

An Hachette UK Company
www.hachette.co.uk
www.hachettechildrens.co.uk

Printed and bound in China

MIX
Paper from
responsible sources
FSC® C104740

Contents

What Is Mental Well-being?   4

Your Mind Matters   6

What Are Mental Health Problems?   8

Stress and Anxiety   10

Dealing With Change   12

It's Good to Talk   14

Love and Affection   16

Give Your Self-Esteem a Boost!   18

Nurturing Your Mental Well-being   20

What Is Mindfulness?   22

Mindfulness Matters   24

Mindfulness Activities   26

Top Tips!   28

Parents' and Teachers' Notes   30

Glossary and Index   32

What Is Mental Well-being?

You can't see mental well-being but you can feel it. Your mental well-being is all about how you think and feel. Some people call it 'mental health' or 'emotional well-being'.

Having good mental health doesn't mean being happy all the time. We all experience feelings of anger, sadness, fear and frustration. These feelings are perfectly normal. Mental well-being comes from finding positive ways to manage these feelings.

Your Mind Matters

Your mental well-being is just as important as your physical health. Good mental health helps you feel happy about yourself. It helps you cope with the everyday pressures of life. Part of being healthy is about understanding your own mental well-being.

Good mental health allows you to think clearly, have good relationships with your family and friends and learn new skills every day. It helps develop your self-confidence and self-esteem, too.

What Are Mental Health Problems?

Mental health problems are thoughts and feelings that can change the way you feel, think and behave. It can be frightening to think you have a mental health problem but it shouldn't be ignored.

Stress, anxiety and depression are all examples of mental health problems. Poor mental health can make you feel as bad as any other illness. Finding ways to deal with a problem can stop it getting worse, so that you can continue to enjoy life.

Stress and Anxiety

Everybody will feel anxious and stressed at some stage in his or her life. You might have felt anxious when you started school or if you have ever moved house. This anxiety and stress usually goes away after a little while.

If these feelings don't disappear, it can affect your mental well-being, your confidence and your self-esteem. You may become sad or angry and you might have difficulty sleeping. It's time to get some help.

Dealing With Change

We all deal with different situations in our lives differently. Most changes in life don't lead to mental health problems. But sometimes an event can trigger thoughts and feelings that lead to poor mental health.

For example, some children may feel excited about the arrival of a new brother or sister. Others may feel anxious about the changes to their home environment and will need to find ways to cope.

It's Good To Talk

Talking about your thoughts and feelings is an important way of looking after your mental well-being. If you are anxious or worried about anything, reassurance from your family and friends can help you deal with your feelings.

If you still feel anxious, it's a good idea to get some professional help. The first place to start is to talk to your doctor. There are also helplines, such as Young Minds, that offer advice and support.

Love and Affection

Your family and friends play an important part in your mental well-being. Human beings need secure and safe relationships to grow, learn and have fun.

The people you meet at home and at school help you understand the world, its cultures and its rules. As you grow up, you build a sense of your place within this world. Your mental well-being helps you feel confident about how you fit in.

Give Your Self-Esteem a Boost!

Self-esteem is how you see yourself. Having low self-esteem can affect your mental health. What affects self-esteem is different for everyone. An experience such as bullying, a mental health problem like stress or a difficult relationship can affect someone's self-esteem.

Giving your self-esteem a boost will boost your mental well-being, too! Try and focus on positive things in your life, such as your friends and any hobbies you enjoy. You could then try writing down a list of your achievements or talking to a friend or loved one.

Nurturing Your Mental Well-being

There are things that you can do to keep mentally well. Here is a list of ways to look after your mental health:

Make time to play and do something you enjoy.

Look after your body by exercising each day.

Eat a balanced diet, including lots of fresh fruit and vegetables.

Spend time with close friends and family who help you feel good about yourself.

Get a good night's sleep to rest your body and your mind.

These things will help you have the strength and resilience to cope with life's stresses, as well as find ways to solve problems.

What is Mindfulness?

One way of looking after your mental well-being is to practise mindfulness. This means learning to focus on the present, rather than worrying about what has happened or what might happen.

Mindfulness exercises help you to focus on your breathing, the sensations in your body and your thoughts and feelings, as well as everyday activities, such as eating and walking.

Mindfulness Matters

At first, it can be difficult not to let your mind wander when you practise mindfulness. There is always something to think about! But, with time, you can learn to hold your attention for longer.

Thinking without being mindful

Stimulus　　　　**Reaction**　　　　**Reaction**

Thinking whilst being mindful

Stimulus　　　　**Reaction**　　　　**Reaction**

Mindfulness can help you concentrate and think more clearly, as well as feel less stressed and anxious. It can even help some people feel less depressed. This can all have a positive effect on your mental well-being.

Mindfulness Activities

Colouring calms the brain and helps the mind focus on one task. The best bit is that it can be done wherever you like. All you need is a colouring book and some pencils!

Mindful posing is another activity you can try at home. Doing funny poses, such as pretending to be a superhero can help you pay more attention to your body and its sensations as you strike a pose!

Go out for a walk and look for as many birds, insects and animals as you can. This uses all your senses and helps you focus on the present.

You could even look for the colours of the rainbow on your walk. Try and find objects that represent each colour. Some colours will be harder to find than others!

Top Tips!

Talking about your feelings isn't a sign of weakness. Having someone listen can give you the support you need.

Your mind needs vitamins and nutrients to keep well. A balanced diet will not only help your body but your mind, too.

Make time for yourself. Some 'me time' can reduce stress and make you feel happier.

Doing a little exercise every day will boost your self-esteem, help you sleep, help you concentrate and make you feel better.

Don't be afraid to ask for help.

Do something you are good at and that you enjoy. This will boost your self-esteem, help you forget your worries and lift your mood.

Parents' and Teachers' Notes

This book is designed for children to begin to learn about the importance of being healthy, and the ways in which we can look after our mental well-being. Read the book with children either individually or in groups. Don't forget to talk about the pictures as you go.

Mental health is just as important as physical health. It affects your thoughts and feelings, your relationships and even how you see yourself. Understanding about mental health is very important. Here are some discussion topics to encourage further thinking about mental well-being:

 Talk about the word 'healthy'. What do you think it means to be mentally healthy?

 Can you think of three ways you can look after your mental health?

 What advice would you give to someone suffering with low self-esteem?

 Mindfulness is one way to look after your mental well-being. Does it seem like something you might want to try?

Activities you can do:

 Grab a colouring book and some pencils and relax while you colour in a favourite picture.

 Have a go at the Mindfulness Jar activity. Fill a jar with water. Add some glitter glue and put the lid back on. Shake the jar. Imagine the glitter is your thoughts and feelings when you are worried or anxious. The pieces are hard to see clearly. When you feel anxious, it's hard to think clearly sometimes, too. Now, put down the jar and watch the glitter settle as the water clears. Your mind works in the same way. Once your thoughts start to settle, you can see things more clearly.

Further reading

Mindful Me: Breath by Breath: A Mindfulness Guide to Feeling Calm by Paul Christelis and Elisa Paganelli (Wayland, 2018)

Healthy for Life: Self-esteem and Mental Health by Anna Claybourne (Franklin Watts, 2016)

Glossary

culture the ideas, customs and way of life of a particular group of people. There are lots of different cultures around the world.

depression a feeling of great sadness and dejection. It is a medical illness so if you feel very depressed you should seek medical help.

environment the surroundings in which a person, animal or plant lives

mental health a person's emotional and mental well-being

physical health the health and well-being of a person's body

professional someone who is an exert in a particular field, such as a doctor or counsellor

resilience being able to recover quickly after a tough experience

self-confidence a feeling of trust in your abilities, qualities and opinions

self-esteem a feeling of confidence and happiness in your own worth as a person

trigger an event that causes a particular situation or feeling

Index

anxiety 9, 10, 14, 15, 25

bullying 18

depression 9, 25
diet 20
doctor 15

emotional well- being 4
exercise 20

family 16, 21
feelings 5, 8, 11, 14, 23
friends 16, 19, 21

hobbies 19
home 12, 13, 17

illness 9

mindfulness, 22, 23, 24, 25, 26, 27
moving house 10

physical health 6, 20

relationships 7, 16, 18

school 10, 17

self-confidence 7, 11, 17
self-esteem 7, 11, 18,19
sleep 11, 21
stress 9, 10, 18, 25

talking 14, 15

worries 14